Struck by Jesus

*Thanks to Jane for
loving support and
always sound advice.*

*Thanks to Andy Dakin of
Christchurch Clifton Drama Group
for 'To Coin a Phrase' script.*

*And to the following
for their excellent
editorial advice:*

*Jane Blazeby
Sue Doggett
Pete Halestrap
Jane Norman
James Traynar
Anna Williams*

Lightning BOLTS

STRUCK BY JESUS

NICK JONES

◆》The Bible Reading Fellowship

Text and illustrations copyright
© 1995 Nick Jones

The author assertes the moral right
to be identified as the author of this work.

Published by
The Bible Reading Fellowship
Peter's Way, Sandy Lane West,
Oxford, England
ISBN 0 7459 3085 9

First edition 1995
10 9 8 7 6 5 4 3 2 1

All rights reserved

Acknowledgments

Scripture quoted from the **Good News Bible**,
published by The Bible Societies/HarperCollins
Publishers Ltd., UK, © American Bible Society,
1966, 1971, 1976, 1992

Cover photograph: Zefa UK

A catalogue record for this book is available
from the British Library

**Printed and bound in Great Britain
by Cox and Wyman Ltd, Reading**

Introduction

Welcome to Mark's Gospel,

Mark's Gospel is the earliest account we have of the life of Jesus. Mark wrote his short 'report' about Jesus' life because he had been really struck by Jesus, and wanted his readers to meet this striking man too. So, if you want to find out what Jesus was like and get to know him for yourself, Mark's Gospel is the book to read.

I have split the Gospel into seventy bite-sized chunks that you can read each day for ten weeks. Each day's reading includes an introduction to the passage, thought-provoking ideas or activities to help you get your mind round its meaning, as well as things to pray about or ponder. For each reading I have written out the key verse just in case you don't have time to read the whole passage.

Getting Started

Each day find yourself a quiet spot where you won't be disturbed for five minutes or so. This can be at any time of the day or night. I find that before breakfast is best but you may prefer to read Mark on the bus into school, in the bath, or in bed. Do whatever you find easiest. Settle down with your copy of Mark, this book and a biro and turn to day 1's reading (each daily reading is numbered at the top). Ask God to help you understand the passage and then follow the instructions on the page. When you've finished you can tick the box next to the day number.

I hope that you really enjoy getting to know Jesus and that he makes his mark on you. I did, and he has.

Nick

*The voice of the Lord strikes
with flashes of lightning.*

Psalm 29:7 (NIV)

Straight in there

1

Read: Mark chapter 1 verses 1–8

This is the Good News about Jesus Christ, the Son of God.
Mark 1:1

Mark kicks off his Gospel by explaining that his book is about Jesus, the Son of God. That is a pretty dramatic introduction. He doesn't start by saying, 'Once upon a time . . .' or 'Hello and welcome to the story of . . .' or even with an explanation of how he came to know about Jesus. He gets straight to the point of his book. That's what Mark's Gospel is like all the way through; the straight facts and no waffle.

How do you feel about finding out the good news about Jesus? (tick one)

☐ **Raring to go**—no one's going to stop me now.

☐ **Pretty excited**—I mean you don't get this kind of opportunity every day.

☐ **Cool, calm & collected**—I'm ready to examine the evidence for myself.

☐ **I'll give it a try**—at least for a few days.

Pray this
'Dear God, help me to understand the good news about Jesus as I read Mark's book over the next few weeks.'

The nod from God

2

Read: Mark chapter 1 verses 9–13

A voice came from heaven, 'You are my own dear Son. I am pleased with you.'

Mark 1:11

Yesterday we read what Mark and John had to say about Jesus. Today we meet him for the first time and hear what the Big Boss has to say.

Write your version of God's words to Jesus in this speech bubble.

Ponder this

God made it clear to everyone who was within ear shot of the River Jordan that Jesus was his Son and that he was pleased with him. Is God saying anything to you about Jesus in this passage? Why don't you talk to him about it?

Head hunting

3

Read: Mark chapter 1 verses 14–20

As Jesus walked along the shore of Lake Galilee, he saw two fishermen, Simon and his brother Andrew, catching fish with a net. Jesus said to them, 'Come with me, and I will teach you to catch people.'

Mark 1:16–17

Mark tells us that one of the first things that Jesus did was get together a team to help him 'catch people' for God. If you were getting together a team to change the world, which kind of people would you head-hunt? Mark with an 'X' the ones that would be key people in your team.

CANDIDATES	X
Advertising Experts	
Religious Leaders	
Public Relations Consultants	
Buisness men & women	
Farmers	
Public Speakers	
Road Sweepers	
Other	

Ponder this

When choosing his team Jesus didn't go for the kind of people you might expect. It didn't matter to him what 'job' his followers did, or whether they were 'important' people or not. The only thing that counted was whether they were prepared to follow him. That is great news because it means Jesus can use anybody in his team; even you and me, so long as we are willing to go with him. Why don't you have a word with him about this?

No messing

4

Read: Mark chapter 1 verses 21–28

The people who heard Jesus were amazed at the way he taught, for he wasn't like the teachers of the Law; instead, he taught with authority.

Mark 1:22

Right from the beginning of Jesus' campaign it was obvious that there was something very different about him. He knew what he was talking about and he knew what he was doing; there was no messing with Jesus.

Write a short poem or limerick that sums up what happened in this passage. Here's one I made up earlier.

When Jesus was preaching in Galilee
He astounded the vast majority
They clearly knew
What he said was true
'Cos he spoke with a real authority

Time for everyone

5

Read: Mark chapter 1 verses 29–34

After the sun had set and evening had come, people brought to Jesus all the sick and those who had demons... Jesus healed many who were sick with all kinds of diseases.

Mark 1:32, 34

In this passage we see that Jesus was now in real demand. The news about him had spread fast. Everyone wanted something from Jesus and he wanted to help every one of them.

Have you ever queued for the signature of a famous person? How did you feel as you waited in the queue? Did you get the signature or did they get fed up with fans before your turn came? Jot your memories down here.

The people who were queuing to see Jesus must have been even more desperate to see him because they weren't just hoping for an autograph but to be healed of their illnesses.

When they realized that Jesus' minders weren't going to say, 'That's enough now' and hustle him off into his waiting limmo they must have been very relieved. Jesus made sure he got to see every person who was waiting to talk to him.

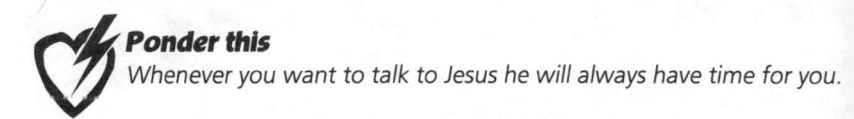

Ponder this

Whenever you want to talk to Jesus he will always have time for you.

Top priority

6 □

Read: Mark chapter 1 verses 35–39

Very early the next morning, long before daylight, Jesus got up and left the house. He went out of the town to a lonely place, where he prayed.

Mark 1:35

Verse 35 gives us a glimpse of how incredibly important it was for Jesus to have time to talk to his Father God. Jesus must have been exhausted after a very busy day, but a lie-in the next morning wasn't on the cards. Instead he set his alarm well before 4 a.m. and slipped off to a place where he could talk to God without being disturbed.

When my wife Jane and I are very busy, we sometimes don't get round to talking to each other; we are both too caught up in our own worlds. When that happens we don't get on so well. It is like that with all relationships and that is why talking to God was so important to Jesus.

Jot down some suggestions of the things that Jesus and God might have talked about.

....

....

....

....

Well God, what's the plan for today?

Pray this
Why don't you talk to God about the things on your list?

12

The loving touch

7

Read: Mark chapter 1 verses 40–45

A man suffering from a dreaded skin-disease came to Jesus, knelt down, and begged him for help. 'If you want to,' he said, 'you can make me clean.' Jesus was filled with pity, and stretched out his hand and touched him. 'I do want to,' he answered. 'Be clean!'

Mark 1:40–41

This man suffering from a dreaded skin-disease was probably a leper. Everyone was terrified of catching this awful disease so lepers had to live on their own, well away from other people. This guy must have been really desperate when he came to Jesus.

What would you do if this leper came up to you asking for help? (tick one)

☐ *Run away as fast as you could, screaming, 'Get away from me you repulsive man.'*

☐ *Pass out. (thud)*

☐ *Smile sweetly and say, 'I'm terribly sorry but my parents told me never to speak to lepers.'*

☐ *Chuck fifty pence at him and walk away feeling guilty.*

☐ *Invite him home to tea.*

Ponder this

Because Jesus cared about this poor man and longed to help him, he ignored all the risks to himself and touched him. That must have been the first time the leper had been touched by a non-leper in years, and must have made as much difference to his life as actually being healed.

Forgiven

8
☐

Read: Mark chapter 2 verses 1–12

The Son of Man [Jesus] has authority on earth to forgive sins.

Mark 2:10

At the time of Jesus people believed that illness was a punishment from God for the wrong things that they had done. This paralysed man was very ill and must have felt that he was in big trouble with God. He was a prisoner of both his paralysis and his guilt. But he discovered that Jesus has authority to forgive sins and loves to set people free from whatever is spoiling their lives. He'd like to do that for you too.

In the chains write down anything that you feel guilty about; maybe things that you wish you hadn't done or things that you should have done but didn't.

Pray this

Ask Jesus to forgive you for these things and set you free from the guilt that you may feel. I promise you that he will, so don't forget to say thanks.

14

'Scum dinner!'

9

Read: Mark chapter 2 verses 13–17

Jesus answered, '... I have not come to call respectable people, but outcasts.'

Mark 2:17

Let's face it, we can all think of people everyone loves to hate or at least look down on: class nerds, school bullies and kids who are 'just a bit different'. It was like that in Jesus' time too. In his day everyone hated tax collectors, prostitutes, lepers and anyone who was not quite like them. They were really shocked and scandalized when Jesus went out of his way to have dinner with the 'scum of their society'.

If Jesus was holding a dinner today, whom would he invite from your school? Jot their names on the table plan below.

Ponder this

Sometimes we may think we are better than other people, but, when it comes to the crunch, not one of us 'deserves' Jesus' help and friendship. But he gives it to us anyway, even though we don't deserve it, because he loves us so much.

Old & new

10

Read: Mark chapter 2 verses 18–22

Jesus said, 'New wine must be poured into fresh wineskins.'

Mark 2:22

The Jewish religious leaders (Pharisees) didn't like the way Jesus refused to do things their way. All through Mark's Gospel they have got their knives out for him and here are complaining that he didn't 'fast' or go without food. So why didn't Jesus tow the line and keep them happy? Well, using the visual aids of the coat and the wineskins, Jesus explained that when he is at work, things need to change. He is like sparkling new wine, fizzing away. (In those days they didn't have wine bottles and used animal skins instead.) Putting sparkling new wine into a dry skin would burst it and both would be wasted.

It is like that with us. It is no good asking Jesus to come and live in us if we are not prepared to change our lifestyle. Jesus wants us to be new and elastic and ready to let him change us. Not dry, set in our ways and just the same as we were before.

Think of one thing that Jesus might want to change in your life. Write it here.

....

....

Pray this
Ask Jesus to help you be new and elastic and ready to change.

Law v love

11

Read: Mark chapter 2 verse 23—chapter 3 verse 6

Jesus concluded, 'The Sabbath was made for the good of human beings; they were not made for the Sabbath.'
Mark 2:27

The Jewish leaders believed that you shouldn't do any kind of work on the Sabbath (a special day like Sunday). Picking corn and healing someone were both definitely work and they were hoping that Jesus would break their rules so that they would have a reason to have him bumped off. Jesus obviously thought it was much more important to help someone in need than to keep these 'religious rules', even if in doing so he was digging his own grave.

When I was a teenager I really loved going to my youth group and looked forward to it every week. Occasionally something would come up, perhaps the visit of some relatives, which meant I couldn't go to the group. This would annoy me because I thought it was more important for me to be at the youth group than with relatives that I hardly even knew! If I had followed Jesus' example I would have realized that showing love to other people is much more important than keeping my own habits or rules, however good they may be in themselves.

Ponder this

Do you ever find that there is a conflict between showing love to friends, relatives or people in need, and doing what you want? Why don't you discuss it with God now?

Jesus fever

12

Read: Mark chapter 3 verses 7–12

Jesus and his disciples went away to Lake Galilee, and a large crowd followed him… All these people came to Jesus because they had heard of the things he was doing.

Mark 3:7–8

The people in this crowd just couldn't get enough of Jesus. They desperately wanted to be near him, to hear what he had to say and to get to know him better. It is as if they had 'Jesus fever'. They felt very passionately about him and were 'red hot' for Jesus.

Have you caught Jesus fever yet? Will nothing stop you getting more of him or are you distinctly frosty towards this guy? Use the thermometer below to indicate how lukewarm or on-fire you are.

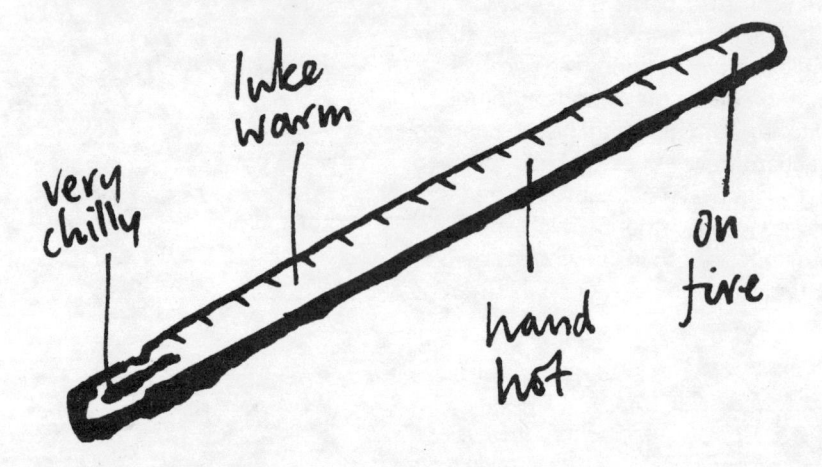

(Thermometer with markings: very chilly | luke warm | hand hot | on fire)

Pray this
Why not talk to Jesus about how you feel about him? He will warm you up if you want him to.

Team talk

13

Read: Mark chapter 3 verses 13–19

Then Jesus went up a hill and called to himself the men he wanted. They came to him, and he chose twelve, whom he named apostles. 'I have chosen you to be with me,' he told them. 'I will also send you out to preach, and you will have authority to drive out demons.'

Mark 3:13-15

Jesus got together a team because he wanted friends and needed people to help him spread his message about; there were no newspapers, books or TV in those days. This passage tells us some important things about being in Jesus' team.

1 **We are to be his friends.**

2 **We are to pass the good news about Jesus on to others.**

3 **We will have his power to help us live for him. Put a cross somewhere on the three lines to show how you are doing on each.**

I don't know Jesus yet.	———————————	I'm best friends with Jesus.
No one knows I'm a Christian.	———————————	My friends know I follow Jesus.
I don't think Jesus helps me.	———————————	Jesus helps me a lot.

Ponder this

Jesus would really like you to get to know him better and to have you in his team. Why not talk to him about this now.

Good & evil

14

Read: Mark chapter 3 verses 20–30

So Jesus said, 'How can Satan drive out Satan?'
Mark 3:23

Jesus gets a lot of hassle in these verses, first from his family who thought he'd gone mad, and secondly from the Jews who said that he was working for the devil! That was a crazy thing to say, as Jesus pointed out. He explained that he couldn't possibly be working for the devil as the things he was doing were hurting the devil and destroying the powers of evil.

Jesus saw a massive battle between good and evil going on in the world. It is still going on now. On the battle-lines below jot down some of the ways that good and evil show themselves in the world today.

```
G _____          E _____
O _____          V _____
O _____          I _____
D _____          L _____
```

Ponder this

Why not ask God to help you play your part in defeating evil today.
CLUE: Start with something small that you can do in your own life, like stop criticizing your brother or sister. Write it out here.

....

Family values

15

Read: Mark chapter 3 verses 31–35

Jesus said, 'Whoever does what God wants him to do is my brother, my sister, my mother.'

Mark 3:35

According to Jesus, membership of God's family isn't a question of shared blood links, something you get from your parents and have in your genes. It's a question of shared values. The most important thing that the members of God's family have in common is that they all do what God wants.

If you are trying to live your life in the way that God wants then you're a member of God's massive family. You've now got quite a few brothers and sisters around.

Fill in your name on this family tree and the names of a few of your brothers and sisters.

Ponder this

Your parents, as well as being your Mum and Dad, could also be your brother and sister. Weird *huh*?!

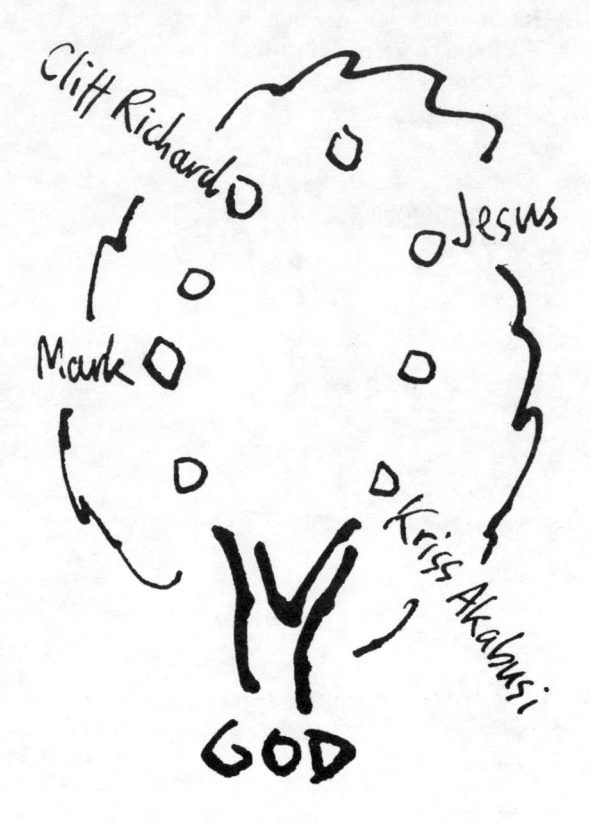

(Family tree shows: Cliff Richard, Jesus, Mark, Kriss Akabusi, GOD)

Sowing stories

16

Read: Mark chapter 4 verses 1–12

Jesus used parables to teach them many things.
Mark 4:2

Jesus had a really smart way of teaching people about God. He used stories about everyday things to make important points about the kingdom of God. Some people would just think that these were nice stories and not understand their deeper meaning. Others who were more open to what God wanted to say to them would really think about the meaning of the story and then act on it. The 'parable' would suddenly give them a glimpse of God, rather as a streak of lightning suddenly lights up the sky.

We'll think about what the parable of the sower means tomorrow, but why not try and invent a parable to make the point that 'God loves everyone.'

Ponder this
If you are anything like me you would have found making up a parable quite hard. The amazing thing is that Jesus made his stories up as he went along! Now that is pretty clever.

Growing up?

17

Read: Mark chapter 4 verses 13–20

Jesus explained, 'The sower sows God's message.'
Mark 4:14

The parable of the sower is all about what people do with the good news about Jesus. Round the pictures below, try and explain what the four types of ground tell us about the way in which people respond to God's message.

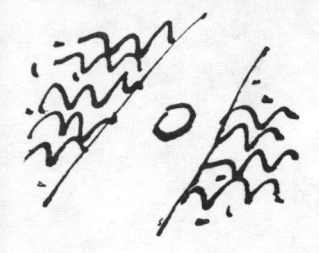

Ponder this
Where do you fit into the story? Why not talk to God about it and ask him to help you produce a good crop.

Pass it on

18

Read: Mark chapter 4 verses 21–25

Jesus continued, 'Does anyone ever bring in a lamp and put it under a bowl or under the bed? Doesn't he put it on the lampstand?'

Mark 4:21

Lamps are for lighting rooms and not for hiding under the bed or under a bowl. (Though I expect you have probably read with a torch under the bed clothes so no one can see that you are not asleep.) The point here is that the truth, like light, is meant to be seen. If you are madly in love you want other people to know. If you discovered a cure for Aids, you wouldn't keep it to yourself but would make sure that it was widely used. It is like that with Jesus. When we discover the good news about Jesus for ourselves it is only natural for us to want to pass it on so other people can enjoy it for themselves too.

Pray this
Don't worry if you don't understand all the ideas in this passage. God will help you understand the truth about him slowly and at just the right speed. But why not ask him to help you pass on the truths about Jesus that you do understand?

24

Hidden energy

19

Read: Mark chapter 4 verses 26–34

Jesus went on to say, 'The Kingdom of God is like this. A man scatters seed in his field. He sleeps at night, is up and about during the day, and all the while the seeds are sprouting and growing. Yet he does not know how it happens.

Mark 4:26–27

Jesus wanted to tell his listeners about the kingdom of God. The kingdom of God means the reign of God—the day when God's will is done as perfectly on earth as it is in heaven. Explaining that isn't easy, so, surprise surprise, Jesus uses a parallel illustration or 'parable' to make his point. He says the kingdom of God is like a crop that grows naturally even when the farmer is asleep.

Why a crop or plant? Well, you and I can't make a plant grow, we can't see a plant grow but they grow all the same. We may not feel that God is making the world a better place but slowly and surely he is. God's kingdom is coming just as surely and quietly as plants grow.

Ponder this

Next time you feel worried about the mess the world is in remember that God's kingdom is on its way even if you can't see it happening.

Unrufflable

20

Read: Mark chapter 4 verses 35–41

Jesus stood up and commanded the wind, 'Be quiet!' and he said to the waves, 'Be still!' The wind died down, and there was a great calm.

Mark 4:39

You may think Harrison Ford is top of the unrufflable ratings but take a look at this man Jesus and think again. He's quietly taking forty winks while his experienced fishermen friends are wetting their pants at the prospect of an imminent close encounter with the sea bed.

Why do you think Jesus can be so cool in such a dangerous situation?

....

How do you fare in a crisis? Do you...

☐ *panic*

☐ *grit your teeth and pray*

☐ *run away*

☐ *wish you were elsewhere*

☐ *take control and triumph*

Ponder this

When the disciples realized that Jesus would look after them, things didn't seem so bad. So next time you think your number's up, or you are unhappy, swamped by problems or just plain scared, remember that Jesus is with you and has a knack for solving problems; then things won't seem half so bad. Honest!

Danger zone

21

Read: Mark chapter 5 verses 1–20

When they came to Jesus, they saw the man who used to have a mob of demons in him. He was sitting there in his right mind; and they were all afraid... So they asked Jesus to leave their territory.

Mark 5:15, 17

These bizarre events occur under cover of darkness in a spooky, remote place. At first glance it appears to be Jesus who is in danger but it turns out that it is the evil spirits and the local inhabitants who are really in trouble.

Jesus had no difficulty fixing this man's problem, but the local villagers weren't too happy about it. You might think they would have been glad to have this lunatic off their hands but instead they were terrified and asked Jesus to leave. They were scared of the effect that he might have on their lives as well. You see, Jesus is dangerous; once you have met him, your life will never be the same again. These people didn't want their cosy lives disturbed by a touch of God!

Write a *health warning* for anyone considering meeting up with Jesus. Make sure it covers both the dangers Jesus presents to cosy lifestyles and the great benefits of life with God.

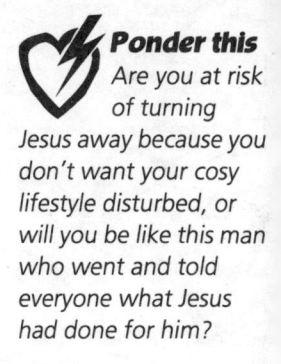

HEALTH WARNING:

Ponder this
Are you at risk of turning Jesus away because you don't want your cosy lifestyle disturbed, or will you be like this man who went and told everyone what Jesus had done for him?

The gentle touch

22

Read: Mark chapter 5 verses 21–43

Jesus took her by the hand and said to her, 'Talitha, koum,' which means, 'Little girl, I tell you to get up!'

Mark 5:41

Some days I am painfully aware of what a mess I make of following Jesus; I hurt other people and let him down. Even though God is not happy with me then, he handles me with the same gentleness as he shows in this passage.

Each of these three characters were in a bit of a state. Next to each one, write down how you think they would have felt about the way in which Jesus helped them.

Ponder this
Is there any problem in your life that could do with the gentle touch of Jesus? Why not talk to him about it?

Breeding contempt

23

Read: Mark chapter 6 verses 1–6a

*The people in Nazareth said, 'Isn't he the carpenter, the son of Mary, and the brother of James and Joseph...?'
...And so they rejected him.*

Mark 6:3

Jesus couldn't do anything for the people of his home town because they didn't believe that he was anyone special. To them he was plain old 'Mary's son'. Having been following Jesus for over ten years I sometimes catch myself being a little bored by the things that he said and did, or rather I take them for granted. That's a dangerous position to be in because, as Jesus found out in Nazareth, he wasn't able to do anything for people like that.

How do you feel about Jesus today? Draw your picture in one box.

☐ **Wide-eyed wonder**—'I'm amazed by the man and can't get enough of him.'

☐ **Increasingly intrigued**—'I'm pretty interested in this bloke Jesus. He's makes some good points and I'm keen to find out more.'

☐ **Frankly frosty**—'OK, so Jesus was a pretty cool bloke but it's still history.'

☐ **Basically bored**—'Heard it all before. Yawn, yawn!'

Pray this
If your response is anything but wide-eyed wonder, why not ask Jesus to open your eyes wide to his wonder?

Mini Js

24

Read: Mark chapter 6 verses 6b–13

Jesus called the twelve disciples together and sent them out two by two.

Mark 6:7

Jesus sent out his disciples to spread the news about him and gave them a chunk of his power so that they could do the kind of things that he did. They became mini Js.

List all the ways described in this passage in which the disciples behaved like Jesus.

1. **verse 7** ....

2. **verse 8** ....

3. **verse 12** ....

4. **verse 13** ....

5. **verse 13** ....

Ponder this

If you are following Jesus then his aim for you is that you become like him. That doesn't mean dressing or looking like him, but behaving in the way in which he behaved and caring for others in the way that he cared.

Hunted herod

25

Read: Mark chapter 6 verses 14–29

When Herod heard about Jesus, he said, 'He is John the Baptist! I had his head cut off, but he has come back to life!'
Mark 6:16

Herod was feeling very guilty about killing John the Baptist. He was hunted by his conscience and it wasn't going to let him rest for one minute.

When Herod heard about Jesus he hoped it was John come back to life. Imagine that you are Herod. What kind of things would you want to say to 'John'? Write him a letter.

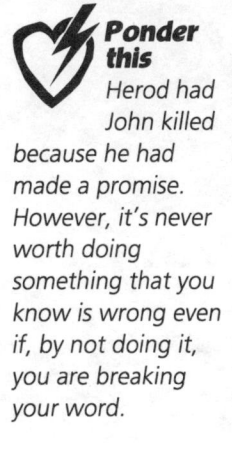

Ponder this

Herod had John killed because he had made a promise. However, it's never worth doing something that you know is wrong even if, by not doing it, you are breaking your word.

Done my bit

26

Read: Mark chapter 6 verses 30–44

When Jesus got out of the boat, he saw this large crowd, and his heart was filled with pity for them, because they were like sheep without a shepherd.

Mark 6:34

The thing about shepherds is that they are never off duty, no matter how tired they are. When people at church ask me for help with projects that they are doing for God, I sometimes think, 'No way—I've done my bit for God already—find someone else.' OK, so I may not put it quite like that, and God doesn't want me to burn out running around doing things for him, but after reading this passage I can't imagine Jesus saying, 'That's all folks! I've done my bit.'

Jesus was aware how badly these people needed his help. They were like 'sheep without a shepherd'. He was the shepherd and he was going to do his bit, no matter what the cost. On the shepherd's job description sheet opposite make a list of the things that a shepherd does for his flock.

SHEPHERD'S JOB DESCRIPTION

1. _____
2. _____
3. _____
4. _____
5. _____

THE SHEEP'S CHARTER

⚡ Ponder this

Jesus is your shepherd and, like all good shepherds, he is never off duty. Which kind of help do you particularly need from him at the moment? Underline it on your list and ask him to give you that help now.

Never fear

27

Read: Mark chapter 6 verses 45–52

Jesus saw that his disciples were straining at the oars... so he came to them, walking on the water... Jesus spoke to them at once, 'Courage!' he said. 'It is I. Don't be afraid!'

Mark 6:48, 50

I must confess that I am frightened quite often. Listening to the news can be frightening if you think about it too much! I am sometimes frightened for my safety and I worry that something terrible will happen to Jane. However, when I realize that Jesus is with me, things don't seem so bad. That's what the disciples needed to discover in this passage; when they realized that Jesus was with them, their difficult situation looked much better.

Think of an image that sums up something that you are afraid of, or worried about, and draw it in the fear bubble below. When you realize that Jesus is with you, and will never leave you, it won't look half so bad. Cut along the dotted line, fold back the page and see why.

Hard hearts

28

Read: Mark chapter 6 verse 53—chapter 7 verse 13

Jesus answered the Pharisees, 'How right Isaiah was when he prophesied about you! You are hypocrites, just as he wrote: "These people, says God, honour me with their words, but their heart is really far away from me."'

Mark 7:6

The Pharisees were slated here by Jesus for honouring God with their lips when their hearts were really far away from him. The Pharisees claimed that they were doing what God wanted, when in fact they were finding clever ways of not doing it. That's hypocrisy and God doesn't like it one little bit.

My definition of hypocrisy is 'Saying or believing one thing and doing the opposite.' Give your life a quick hypocrisy test. Think back over the last week and see if anything you have done has been the opposite of what you believe about following Jesus. For example, you might believe that God wants you to be honest but you have told a few porky-pies. Jot these on the X-ray.

Pray this

Dr God has got X-ray eyes and knows about the things that go on in your head. Why not ask the Doc to forgive you and help you to change. That's his speciality.

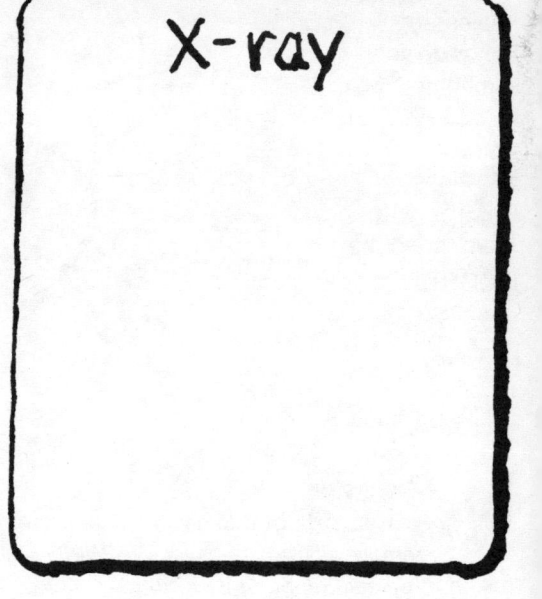

Dirty hearts

29

Read: Mark chapter 7 verses 14–23

Jesus went on to say, 'It is what comes out of a person that makes him unclean. For from the inside, from a person's heart, come the evil ideas which lead him to do immoral things...'

Mark 7:20–21

The Jews believed that if you ate the wrong kind of food or mixed with the wrong kind of people then God would be angry with you because you had made yourself 'unclean'. Jesus is not very impressed with this theory because a person could easily eat the 'right' foods, but still be thinking evil thoughts or kicking the dog, or beating their wife and kids! God is more interested in you and me having 'clean hearts' than looking clean on the outside.

What dirty, unpleasant things do you sometimes find in your heart? (e.g. jealousy or selfishness). Draw or write them round the heart here.

Pray this

Why not ask God to give you a bit of spiritual 'open heart surgery' and remove all the rotten bits. WARNING: This may take some time and it's bound to be painful, but it is worth it!

Everyone welcome

30

Read: Mark chapter 7 verses 24–30

A woman, whose daughter had an evil spirit in her, heard about Jesus and came to him at once and fell at his feet. The woman was a Gentile, born of the region of Phoenicia in Syria.

Mark 7:25–26

One of the things that particularly strikes me about Jesus is the way he always puts his teaching into practice. Yesterday he explained to his disciples that the 'wrong' food or company doesn't make you unclean. This shocked them because the Jews believed that mixing with anyone who wasn't a Jew (a Gentile) was very seriously sinful. In today's passage Jesus puts his teaching into practice by going to visit some Gentiles! Shock! Horror! Gasp! Jesus had given the Jews the first opportunity to hear the good news and now it was open for everyone to hear.

You may feel that Jesus is a bit hard on this woman, but I think you can be fairly sure that he had a mighty big twinkle in his eye as he spoke these teasing words.

How good are you at following Jesus' example in caring about everyone? If you want to find out, complete the 'So just how compassionate are you?' quiz on the next three pages. Just tick whichever answer best describes what you would do in each of the ten situations. Then add up your scores and find out just how compassionate you are.

37

So just how compassionate are you?

1. **Whilst walking down the street with your mates you come across a pink teddy lying in the gutter. What would you do?**
   - [ ] a. Pick it up and put it on the nearest wall.
   - [ ] b. Make a joke about it having lost its way home.
   - [ ] c. Rub its face in the dirt with your heel.
   - [ ] d. Pick it up, take it to the nearest teddy hospital and phone the missing bear line.

2. **You walk into the school canteen with your mates and see a new boy or girl sitting on their own. What would you do?**
   - [ ] a. Get your friends to join you and go and sit on the new person's table.
   - [ ] b. Go up to them, throw your arms round them and invite them home for tea.
   - [ ] c. Sit with your mates on the next table and flick food at them.
   - [ ] d. Nothing. What do you think I am? A member of the school governor's welcoming committee!?

3. **The teacher trainee who is on a placement at your school suddenly loses control of your class. What would you do?**
   - [ ] a. Make the most of a rare opportunity. Waaahooo!
   - [ ] b. Get on with whatever I was meant to be doing.
   - [ ] c. Try and shut my mates up. These poor teacher trainee's deserve a bit of support!
   - [ ] d. Have a good natter with my friends. Well, at least I'm not rioting!

4. **After the evening news there is an emergency appeal for a flood in Bangladesh. What would you do?**
   - [ ] a. Shed a few tears at the upsetting pictures (particularly the baby with big eyes).
   - [ ] b. Send some money off there and then. No time like the present.
   - [ ] c. Think that you must get round to seeing if you have any spare money in your piggy bank.
   - [ ] d. Thank your parents that you don't live in Bangladesh.

5. **You discover that your little bro is being bullied at school. How would you react?**
   - [ ] a. Tell him that he should always tell you about it and try and persuade him to talk to his teachers.
   - [ ] b. Kick the stuffing out of the pigs who are picking on little bro.

☐ c. *Have a word with his friends and see if they can help.*

☐ d. *Think that it serves the little brat right.*

6. Your best friend's parents are splitting up and it is making your friend very moody and difficult to cope with. What would you do?

☐ a. *Hang in there with them even if it's tough.*

☐ b. *Give myself a break. Heck, as if I haven't got enough problems of my own to cope with.*

☐ c. *Suggest they see a psychiatrist fast.*

☐ d. *Try not to get moody too.*

7. Your Mum's had a bad day, has a terrible headache and asks you to turn your music right down. What would you do?

☐ a. *Turn it down without making a fuss, but fume for at least two minutes.*

☐ b. *Turn it off completely. Well, there is no point in getting stressed about such fleeting matters.*

☐ c. *Give her a sympathetic smile, but leave that vol. level just about where it was. Can't let parents interfere with my cultural education!*

☐ d. *Glare at her, slam the door and then turn it down with a sigh.*

8. You were really looking forward to the disco on Saturday night but in the afternoon your mum & dad announce that you are going to visit your gran who hasn't been too well. How would you react?

☐ a. *Sigh graciously and start looking forward to the next disco. Well, I'm just glad Gran is better.*

☐ b. *Suggest you write a nice note for them to take to Gran. Hey, I could even buy some flowers. How does that sound Mum?*

☐ c. *Dream on Mum & Dad. I know this is just a ploy to stop me having fun. Well, I'm not falling for it.*

☐ d. *Kick up one hell of a fuss and wish (but not say) that Gran didn't exist.*

9. On the way into Maths one day the class wally comes up to you and asks to sit next to you. What would you say?

☐ a. *'What! Who do you think I am? Mother Teresa? Listen mate, I've got my image to think about!'*

☐ b. *'I'm not sure it's a good idea. Sitting on your own kind'a suits you. Honest!'*

☐ c. *Nothing. 'Oh, I thought you were talking to someone else. If you must.'*

☐ d. *'Yeah of course. I would be really pleased; we can work together.'*

10. *Your mates have really got it in for a member of your class. OK, so you don't particularly like this person, but your mates are being a bit over-the-top. What would you do?*

☐ a. Let your hair down and join in. Well, it's only a bit of fun really.
☐ b. Nothing. Best to keep one's head down in case they pick on me next.
☐ c. Tell them to stop being so juvenile. I mean haven't they got anything better to do with their time!?
☐ d. Try to put in a good word here and there. If only for the sake of balance.

Now add up your scores and find out how you've done:

1. a2 b1 c0 d3
2. a3 b2 c0 d1
3. a0 b2 c3 d1
4. a1 b3 c2 d0
5. a3 b1 c2 d0
6. a3 b0 c1 d2
7. a2 b3 c0 d1
8. a3 b2 c1 d0
9. a0 b1 c2 d3
10. a0 b1 c3 d2

Compassion bypass (0—7)

Well, er, what can I say except that I sure am glad that I'm not related to you. Seriously though, being perhaps just a touch more caring would make quite a difference to the quality of life for those poor souls who have to share living space with you. Try it. It won't kill you!

Compassion capable (8—15)

OK, so you may not feel that you are the world's most compassionate dude but the seeds are there. Let 'em flourish. When on the verge of doing something compassionate, don't hold back but take the plunge and make it a habit.

On the right lines (16—24)

You are emitting healthy doses of compassion which is a mighty good thing. But you've still got room for improvement. (But then you have got years ahead of you to work on your compassion rating.) Just hang in there and let it all flow out. Who cares what those streetwise sassy kids say anyway?

What a saintly soul (25—30)

If you really would do what you've said you would then you are not far away from sainthood. Perhaps you could start giving compassion classes to us beginners. But beware—don't let it go to your head. This is only a silly little quizlet anyway. God might use a different compassion test!

A personal touch

31

Read: Mark chapter 7 verses 31–37

Jesus took the deaf and dumb man off alone, away from the crowd, put his fingers in the man's ears, spat, and touched the man's tongue... At once the man was able to hear.'

Mark 7:33, 35

The way in which Jesus treated this deaf and dumb man shows us just how tender he was with people. Read the passage again and make a list of the things that Jesus did with this man that you haven't seen him do up to this point in Marks's Gospel. CLUE: there are four in verse 33 and one in verse 34.

1. ....

2. ....

3. ....

4. ....

5. ....

This poor chap could not speak or hear; he could only see. Try and imagine how strange that must be. Jesus did not want to frighten him so he took him away from the crowd and explained in a visual way what he was doing. The man would have understood what Jesus meant when he touched him. Jesus could have just healed the man by saying the word but he is much more thoughtful than that.

Mr Considerate

32

Read: Mark chapter 8 verses 1–10

Jesus said, 'I feel sorry for these people, because they have been with me for three days and now have nothing to eat.'

Mark 8:2

What would you do if you were walking down the street and came across an old lady lying in the gutter?

....

Most people prefer not to get involved in other people's troubles. A couple of years ago my Dad, who is now retired, tripped over a paving stone as he walked down the street. He badly twisted his ankle and couldn't walk. The street was very busy and loads of people walked past before anyone stopped to help. It's human not to want to get involved in other people's problems. In this passage, however, we see that it is divine to be moved with compassion and help. Jesus realized that the people had a long walk home and were very hungry, and decided to *do* something about it.

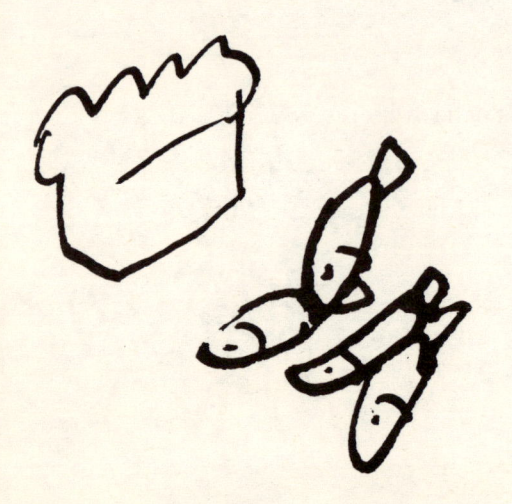

Ponder this

When the disciples pointed out the difficulty of helping, Jesus challenged them to do what they could. Is there anyone whom you know who is in need and whom you could help? Well, get off your backside and try to do what you can! Write out your plan of attack on the blackboard opposite.

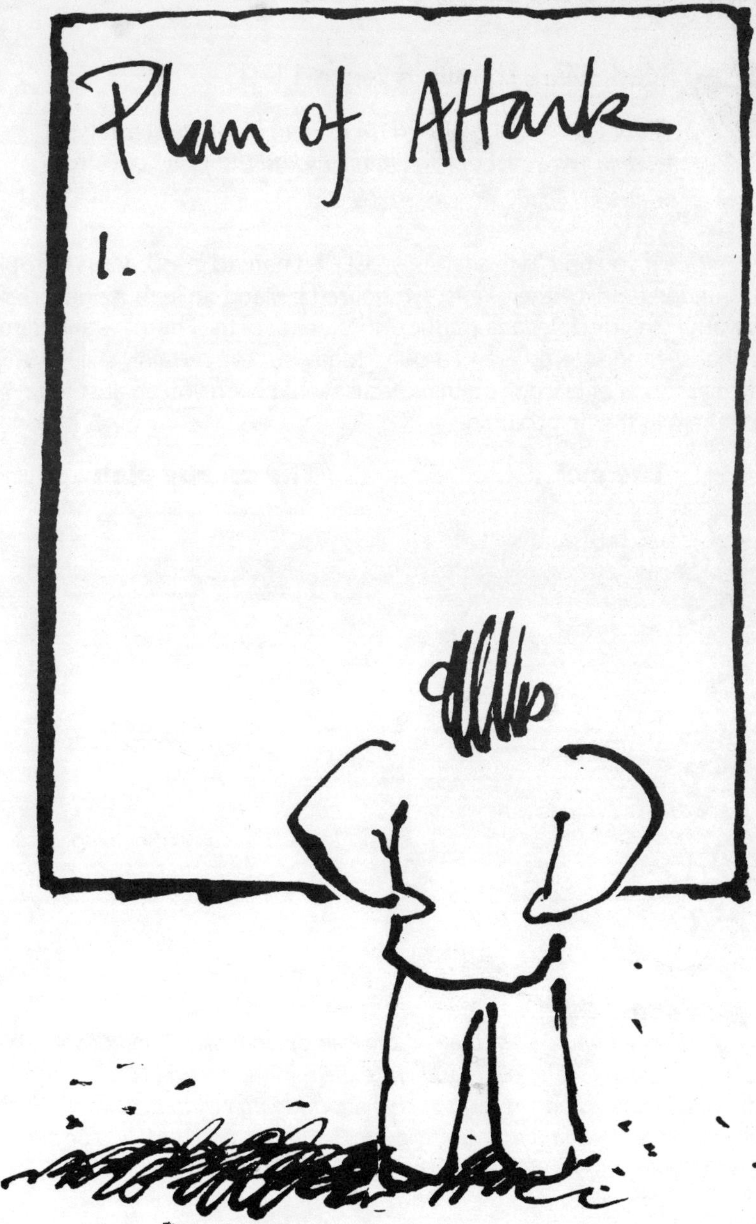
Plan of Attack
1.

The evil influence

33

Read: Mark chapter 8 verses 11–21

'Take care,' Jesus warned them, 'and be on your guard against the yeast of the Pharisees and the yeast of Herod.'

Mark 8:15

Don't worry if you find all this talk of yeast a bit hard to grasp; Jesus' disciples didn't understand it either. Yeast symbolized evil and sin in those days. Jesus was warning his disciples against the evil influence of the Pharisees and Herod. The Pharisees and Herod aren't around today but evil certainly still is. Which particular forms of evil do you think Jesus would warn you against today? Write them in the first column.

The evil	**The escape plan**
....	....
....	....
....	....

Ponder this

How are you going to avoid the evils on your list? Think of some concrete escape plans and write them in the second column next to each evil warning. I know it can be very hard deciding not to do something that all your friends are doing and are trying to get you to do. But if you decide that you don't want to join in, stick to your guns—God is right behind you.

Blindness & sight

34

> Read: Mark chapter 8 verses 22–30
>
> *'What about you?' Jesus asked them. 'Who do you say I am?'*
> Mark 8:29

This is the crunch point of the whole Gospel of Mark. Jesus asks his disciples who they think he is. (Have they twigged yet?) Remember what Mark wrote in the very first sentence of his book? The question is: Have the disciples worked it out for themselves yet? Well, Peter has a flash of inspiration and Jesus is relieved that he is beginning to get somewhere.

But what about you? You have now read half way though Mark's Gospel; from all that you have heard and seen, how would you answer Jesus' question, 'Who do you say I am?'

Draw yourself here or stick in a passport photo and fill in your answer.

Pray this
If you can't quite see who Jesus is, ask God to open your eyes. Sometimes he does it in stages, rather like the healing of the blind man in this passage.

Tough stuff

35

Read: Mark chapter 8 verse 31—chapter 9 verse 1

Jesus said, 'For whoever wants to save his own life will lose it; but whoever loses his life for me and for the gospel will save it.'

Mark 8:35

Jesus never promised that following him would be easy. In fact he said it would be very difficult; 'taking up your cross' means being ready to give your whole life to Jesus! Gulp! Jesus expects his followers to learn to say 'no' to their selfish desires and 'yes' to what he wants them to do.

Make a list of some of the things that you know Jesus wants you to say 'No' to, and another list of the things to which he wants you to say 'Yes'; perhaps 'No' to fighting with your brother and 'Yes' to helping Mum.

Ponder this

If you ask him, Jesus will give you the strength to say 'No' to the things on your 'No' list, and 'Yes' to the things on your 'Yes' list. Try it and you will find that you really start living!

Encouraging

36

Read: Mark chapter 9 verse 2–13

Then a cloud appeared and covered them with its shadow, and a voice came from the cloud, 'This is my own dear Son—listen to him!'

Mark 9:7

To us this seems like a pretty strange business. Jesus and his top three disciples arrive at the summit of some mountain. Jesus starts dazzling, Moses and Elijah show up, the clouds come down and God says a few words. What on earth is going on?

The simplest explanation is that God is giving Jesus and his boys a bit of plain old encouragement. God's top men from the Old Testament are there to pat him on the back and tell him he's going in the right direction. God has some encouraging words for the disciples, and the dazzling transformation that comes over Jesus shows us just how close he was to God.

Ponder this

If Jesus needed a bit of encouraging, so did his disciples and so do those who follow him today. Think of someone you know who is trying to follow Jesus and give them some encouragement next time you see them. You'll find it works wonders.

Fragile faith

37

Read: Mark chapter 9 verses 14–29

Jesus said, 'Everything is possible for the person who has faith.' The father at once cried out, 'I do have faith, but not enough. Help me to have more!'

Mark 9:23–24

In the past there have been times when I have felt let down by other Christians when they have not given me the help or support I needed. This poor man had a similar experience; Jesus' disciples weren't able to help him and that put quite a dent in his faith in God. However, when he finally got to see Jesus he wasn't let down; Jesus healed his son. The point here is that even though there will be times when other followers of Jesus let us down and disappoint us, Jesus never will. He doesn't dent our faith but makes it stronger.

Pray this

Do you ever feel that your faith is a bit fragile? Either way, why not join in with this man's prayer to Jesus, 'I do have faith, but not enough. Help me to have more!' Write out your version in the speech bubble.

Key truths

38

Read: Mark chapter 9 verses 30–41
(focus on verses 30–37)

Jesus taught his disciples, 'The Son of Man will be handed over to those who will kill him. Three days later, however, he will rise to life.'

Mark 9:31

Jesus knew that he was heading fast towards a very unpleasant death. In these verses we see him spending time with his disciples trying to get across to them some key points.

Jot down the key points that you see in the following two verses.

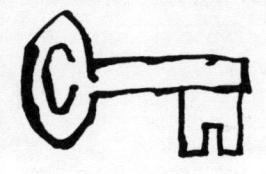

verse 31 ....

verse 35 ....

Ponder this

These keys open the door to 'Life'. Once you accept that Jesus died for you and that God wants you to serve others you will find that you begin to live your life in the way that God intends. These two keys are the keys to happiness. Use 'em!

Serious action

39

Read: Mark chapter 9 verses 42–50

Jesus said, 'If your eye makes you lose your faith, take it out! It is better for you to enter the Kingdom of God with only one eye than to keep both eyes and be thrown into hell.'

Mark 9:47

If you want to do anything well you need to deal ruthlessly with the things that distract or hinder you. I'm an artist and if I want to paint well I have to make sure that I can concentrate 100 per cent. That means switching off the radio. This is exactly the point that Jesus is making here. If you want to live your life well for God you have to deal with the things that distract you. The bit about taking your eye out isn't to be taken literally; what he means is that, if watching horror films is not helping you live for God, then *don't* watch them. If your so-called friends are leading you astray then *don't* hang around with them. The goal of living well for God is definitely worth these sacrifices.

Ponder this
Do you want to live well for God?

Yes ☐   No ☐   Not sure ☐

What one thing most prevents you from living your life really well for God (e.g. a bad habit or friendship)? Work out what you can do to 'cut it off' and write it here.

....
....
....
....

Now that's a weight off my mind.

Hint

It would be a good idea to ask another Christian to help and pray for you. Just telling someone else what you plan to do will make a big difference. Go on! Take the plunge.

Family matters

40

Read: Mark chapter 10 verses 1–12

Jesus said, 'For this reason a man will leave his father and mother and unite with his wife, and the two will become one... No human being then must separate what God has joined together.'

Mark 10:7-9

In the time of Jesus it was considered quite OK for a man to divorce his wife if she just burnt the dinner or if he found someone who he thought was more attractive. Getting married was a bit risky for girls. Your sweet, loving fiancé might not turn out to be quite the husband you expected!

So what does Jesus think about divorce? Well, his views were unpopular then and are unpopular now. He is against it because, as he says, husbands and wives were designed to love each other for the rest of their days.

Pray this

Many people who are reading this will have had first hand experience of divorce, and those who haven't will know someone who has. It's very painful and people going through it need your prayers and support. In fact, parents in general need support. So whether your Mum and Dad are happily married, unhappily divorced, unhappily married or happily separated, or neither married nor divorced, why not use this space to write a prayer for them.

Dear God
About Mum + Dad...

Child's play

41

Read: Mark chapter 10 verses 13–16

Jesus said, 'I assure you that whoever does not receive the Kingdom of God like a little child will never enter it.'

Mark 10:15

Do you ever get fed up with adults treating you like a child or telling you to grow up? Well, having read this passage you can be sure that Jesus would never do that. In fact he's telling any adults who want to be close to God to start 'growing down' and take a few lessons from children about the things that matter to God!

What do you think are the kind of childlike qualities that make children such a good example for adults who want to get to know God better? Make a list of your ideas here.

Pray this

Why not talk to God about your ideas and ask him to help you hang on to those special qualities as you get older.

Wealth warning

42

Read: Mark chapter 10 verses 17–31

Jesus looked round at his disciples and said to them, 'How hard it will be for rich people to enter the Kingdom of God!'

Mark 10:23

You might find today's passage a bit shocking. What's so wrong with having money, so long as it was got fairly, gov? Why is it so hard for rich people to enter the kingdom of God?

Well, the only way in which we can be friends with God is by gratefully accepting his free offer of forgiveness and new life. There is absolutely no way in which we can earn a place in God's kingdom. It's a gift that we don't deserve one little bit. OK?

The reason that money is bad for your spiritual health is that:

1. *It tends to make you trust in yourself; and if you trust in yourself you think you don't need help; and if you think you don't need help God can't help you.*

2. *It's hard not to treasure it and if you treasure it, it's very difficult to treasure God. If you've got that, now turn the page...*

Devise an advertising poster warning of the harm that money can do to people's spiritual health.

Pray this
Dear God, however much money I have now or in the future, please help me to remember that it is only on loan from you.

Now listen 'ere

43

Read: Mark chapter 10 verses 32–34

Once again Jesus took the twelve disciples aside and spoke of the things that were going to happen to him.'

Mark 10:32

I want you to try and imagine that you are one of Jesus' disciples. You have been travelling with him for three years and you are incredibly excited about all that has happened and about what Jesus is going to do in the future. You've seen the miracles, you've heard his teaching and you believe that Jesus is God.

One day Jesus gets you and the other disciples together and says, 'Now listen here, we are on our way to Jerusalem where I am going to be betrayed, condemned to death, mocked, beaten, spat at, whipped and killed. Then, after three days, I will be alive again.' What thoughts would rush through your head as he told you these things. What would you say to him?

thinks *says*

Ponder this

Jesus' disciples didn't have a clue what he was talking about and couldn't understand why it had to be so. But if they had managed to stop him then you and I would never be friends with God. What a terrible thought!

Great goals

44

Read: Mark chapter 10 verses 35–45

Jesus said, 'If one of you wants to become great, he must be the servant of the rest; and if one of you wants to be first, he must be the slave of all.'

Mark 10:43–44

Do you ever imagine yourself as the greatest football player or musician of all time? Do you ever picture yourself as prime minister, or a Blue Peter presenter, or whoever it is that you dream of being? I certainly do. Becoming great like that would involve much hard work, self-promotion, talent and luck.

In today's passage Jesus gives us a very surprising route to greatness. He said, 'If one of you wants to be great, he must be the servant of the rest; and if one of you wants to be first, he must be the slave of all.' That means serving others in whatever we do, whether we are politicians, football players or pupils.

Think of one little thing that you can do to set you on the road to Jesus-style greatness and draw it in the picture frame opposite.

setting out on the road to greatness

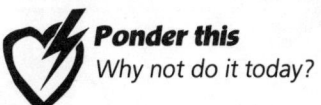

⚡ Ponder this
Why not do it today?

Help me Jesus!

45

Read: Mark chapter 10 verses 46–52

A blind beggar named Bartimaeus... was sitting by the road. When he heard it was Jesus of Nazareth, he began to shout, 'Jesus! Son of David! Take pity on me!'

Mark 10:46–47

A large crowd surrounded Jesus as he walked to Jerusalem and by the wayside was a blind beggar called Bartimaeus. Blind Bart discovered that it was Jesus who was walking past. He realized that this was his *BIG* chance, perhaps his only chance to be cured and, oh boy, did he make sure that Jesus knew he needed his help! He shouted and shouted and despite being told to shut up, he shouted until he succeeded in attracting Jesus' attention.

Blind Bart is a very good example to us: he knew he needed Jesus' help, he was determined to get it; he knew what he wanted Jesus to do for him, and he was ready to do whatever Jesus asked. How do you compare with Blind Bart? Score yourself out of ten for each.

How much do you know you need Jesus' help? ____/10

How determined are you to get Jesus' help? ____/10

How much do you know what you want Jesus to do for you? ____/10

How ready are you to do whatever Jesus asks? ____/10

Pray this
Dear Jesus, you know how much I have scored for each question. Please help me to want to follow you more closely.

Misunderstood

46

Read: Mark chapter 11 verses 1–11

They brought the colt to Jesus, threw their cloaks over the animal, and Jesus got on… The people began to shout, 'Praise God! God bless him who comes in the name of the Lord!'

Mark 11:7, 9

The Jews of Jerusalem were eagerly expecting the Messiah who would flatten the occupying Romans. They were right in thinking that Jesus was the Messiah, but were very wrong about what kind of Messiah he was. He wasn't a king who conquered by war as the crowds proclaim. Instead, he conquered by love and peace; hence the donkey. He was misunderstood.

If you were in the crowd, what kind of things would you have wanted to shout about Jesus as he rode into Jerusalem to die for you? Fill in the speech bubble.

Ponder this
Why not tell Jesus what you would have shouted. He'll appreciate it.

Anger

47

Read: Mark chapter 11 verses 12–25
(focus on verses 15–19)

Jesus went to the Temple and began to drive out all those who were buying and selling... He then taught the people: 'It is written in the Scriptures that God said, "My Temple will be called a house of prayer for the people of all nations." But you have made it a hideout for thieves!'

Mark 11:15, 17

Last week I went to see *Schindler's List*, Stephen Speilberg's film about the extermination of Jews in Nazi Germany. There was one scene that made me particularly angry. The soldiers had just packed hundreds of Jews onto a train taking them to a concentration camp. They had been told that their luggage would follow, but instead it was all unpacked and plundered. Somehow the way in which the Nazis were treating the Jew's possessions symbolized the horrific way in which the Jews themselves were being treated. It made me furious and I wanted to do something.

In a way that's a little bit like what happened when Jesus went into the temple. He was furious at the way in which God's house had been turned into a market and the pilgrims were being ripped off. Oh boy, did he take some serious action!

Ponder this

There is a lot that happens in the world that makes God angry. If it makes him angry, it should make us angry too. Think of one wrong thing that is happening in your school and ask him what he would like you to do about it. Write out what you plan to do here.

....

....

Tricky questions

48

Read: Mark chapter 11 verses 27–33

As Jesus was walking in the Temple, the chief priests... came to him and asked him, 'What right have you to do these things? Who gave you this right?

Mark 11:27–28

The Jewish leaders were a bit miffed about Jesus messing up the temple so they tried to trap him with a question that would get him into trouble whichever way he answered. If he said that he cleared the temple on his own authority, they could arrest him for being a nut case. If he said that he did it on God's authority, they could arrest him for being a blaspheming nut case, because God wouldn't mess up his own temple now, would he? Anyway, Jesus got out of it by giving them a taste of their own medicine.

Going back to the first question, what right do *you* think Jesus had to make such a mess of God's temple?

....

....

If Jesus felt that things needed shaking up in your life would you give him permission?

Yes ☐   **No** ☐   **Not sure** ☐

Ponder this
Even if you aren't too keen on the thought of Jesus shaking up your life, you mustn't worry about it because he knows what he is doing and it will definitely be for the better.

Close to the mark

49

Read: Mark chapter 12 verses 1–12

Then Jesus spoke to them in parables, 'Once there was a man who planted a vineyard...'

Mark 12:1

This is a parable aimed straight at the Jewish leaders and it must have been rather painful. Below on the left are the five main characters in the parable. Jumbled up on the right are the people they represent. Try and match up the people in the story with who they are meant to be. Draw a line connecting them.

1. THE OWNER OF THE VINEYARD   The Jewish Nation A.

2. THE VINEYARD   Jesus B.

3. THE TENANTS   God C.

4. THE OWNER'S SERVANTS   The Jewish Leaders D.

5. THE SON   The Old Testament Prophets E.

Once you have worked out whom the different characters in the story represent, you will be able to understand what Jesus was saying to the Jewish leaders. Check that your answers are correct; they should match up like this: 1–C, 2–A, 3–D, 4–E, 5–B.

Read through the parable again remembering whom the characters represent. Do you get it now?

Yes ☐   No ☐   Not sure ☐

To coin a phrase

50

Read: Mark chapter 12 verses 13–17

So Jesus said, 'Well, then, pay the Emperor what belongs to the Emperor, and pay to God what belongs to God.'

Mark 12:17

Think about this story from the coin's point of view. Here are two coins, 'A' and 'B', talking about it at the bank.

A: It's great to be back at the bank isn't it?

B: Yes, slip me some face.

A: Where have you been?

B: Oh Israel, it was my fifth tour of foreign duty.

A: Israel! That place is the pits. I went there back in AD20 on my second tour, I felt totally out of circulation.

B: Yes, I know what you mean. It's just not well-up, wild and wicked out there. A home tour is what I want next, here in Rome.

A: Yes, sound as a pound. Rome is the ace place to show your face. Well, Caesar's anyway.

B: I really got into some shady deals when I was in Israel . . . just so wicked. It was nearly melt down after the sphinx mat gold bullion robbery. Trouble is, after that sort of experience you get a bad reputation, you are tarnished.

A: You mean you get a heavy 'rep'.

B: Yes, you got it. Israel was such a devaluing experience. You know that nowadays people over there use us to take decisions!

A: What?

B: Yes, they toss us up in the air. I hate it, it puts me in a real spin, then they let you fall on your face and in the middle of all this, and you're not going to believe what I tell you now, they call out 'Bonces or Bums'!

A: Oh, how crude!

B: And depending on which face it is, this determines the decision.

A: That really is over the top! I don't like that Bonce and you know—Why don't they say something like—heads or tails?

B: No. It just hasn't got the same street cred. 'Heads or tails' will never catch on. My worst experience in Israel was when I got jammed in a toilet door for forty days and nights in a Jericho convenience.

A: Talk about being abused.

B: Yes, it was a really wicked time. This geezer wanted to use me to spend a penny.

A: What?

B: Yea, you know 'Do a Denarius'. It was wicked I can tell you. Anyway, just before I came back from Israel, I had this amazing experience.

A: Yea?

B: Yea, I belonged to this real cool dude called Phoenix the Pharisee, and he had me polished every day before he took me out.

A: Hey, smooth!

B: Yea, you got it. I'm so smooth . . . when I'm polished! Anyway, as I was saying, one day we were down in Jerusalem and Phoenix was having a rap with some other dudes when he suddenly flashed me out.

A: You mean 'flashed the cash'?

B: Yea, you got it. And he gave me to a Jew called Jesus.

A: Gave you to a Jew! That is really, really, really wicked!

B: Yea, anyway this man Jesus took hold of me, held me up and said, 'Whose face and name are these?' And then Phoenix and the other dudes said, 'Caesar's', and Jesus said, 'Well then pay to the Emperor what belongs to the Emperor, and pay God what belongs to God.'

A: What happened then?

B: Well, everyone was silent; you could have heard a coin drop.

A: And what about Phoenix?

B: Oh, he looked well narked. Funny though, after Jesus touched me I didn't feel abused and devalued like normal and now I feel different; I feel ready for the big melt down.

A: Oh no! Not reincoination!

B: No, being 'born again' to coin a phrase.

Andy Dakin

Heavenly

51

Read: Mark chapter 12 verses 18–27

Jesus answered them, 'For when the dead rise to life, they will be like angels in heaven and will not marry.'
Mark 12:25

I find it impossible to imagine what heaven will be like. How would you describe it to an interested friend?

....

....

If you are anything like me you might mention all the things that you really enjoy about life on earth such as ice cream and video games and say that heaven will be one-never-ending-chocolate-chip-extra-yummy-triple-layer-sonic-the-hedgehog-game. But if you did that you would be making the same mistake as the Sadducees in this passage. Like you and me, they could only imagine life after death as being a better version of life on earth. Jesus says that is wrong.

Life with God will be infinitely better than a never-ending-chocolate-chip-sonic-the-hedgehog-game (thank goodness), but quite how we don't know. The only clue that Jesus gives us here is that it is all about relationships. Think of one of the relationships that is very special to you. What makes it so special?

Ponder this

Jesus is saying that in heaven our relationship with God will be wonderfully close and our relationships with the rest of God's family will enter a whole new dimension. However, we will have to wait to see quite how.

The meaning of life

52

Read: Mark chapter 12 verses 28–34

Jesus answered, 'Love the Lord your God with all you heart, with all your soul, with all your mind, and with all your strength'... 'Love your neighbour as you love yourself.' There is no other commandment more important than these two.'

Mark 12:30–31

Dear Reader,

I thought I would write you a letter. (Sorry it's not hand written, but, if it was, you wouldn't be able to read it.) Anyway, I'll get straight to the point. I was wondering if you ever lie awake at night thinking about why you are alive? Do you ever find yourself wondering what the point of life is?

Well, in this passage Jesus explains it very clearly. He says that the meaning of life is loving God and loving other people. Read verses 30 and 31 again. It sounds so simple, doesn't it? Well, he's right. Try imagining what the world would be like if everyone loved God and other people with their whole heart. What a different place the world would be! In fact it would be paradise.

I guarantee that you and I will only find true happiness and fulfilment when we fall in love with God and learn to show his love to other people. Why not talk to him about this? He is already in love with you.

Ponder this
The depth of your love for God is to be measured by the way you treat the person you like least.

Nick

Wildly generous

53

> Read: Mark chapter 12 verses 35–44
> (focus on verses 41–44)
>
> *Jesus said, 'I tell you that this poor widow put more in the offering box than all the others. For the others put in what they had to spare of their riches; but she, poor as she is, put in all she had.'*
>
> Mark 12:43-44

The other day my Mum was sorting out the attic and came across lots of letters, notes and presents made out of egg boxes and toilet rolls. My brothers and I had given them to my mum and dad when we were very young. The messages were embarrassingly honest: 'Dear Mummy and Daddy, thank you for being so nice. I love you.' I loved my parents and tried to show it by giving them things. In this passage the poor widow wanted to show God how much she loved him by giving him all she could. It wasn't much money but it meant a lot to God. What a pleasant contrast she makes with those hypocritical teachers of the Law!

It is right to give God presents that show how much we love him and how grateful we are for all he has done for us. But it is not 'how much' we give that makes it special, but rather how much what we give means to us.

Ponder this

If you love God why not give him a present today and make it a habit for life? Work out what you want to give him and draw or describe it here. Doing things for other people and giving money to good causes are both ways of giving presents to God; your gifts don't have to be things that you wrap up!

Tough times ahead

54

Read: Mark chapter 13 verses 1–13
(focus on 9–13)

Jesus said, 'Everyone will hate you because of me. But whoever holds out to the end will be saved.'

Mark 13:13

In chapter 13 Jesus gives his listeners lots of little pictures of things that will happen in the future. It is rather like a complicated jig-saw. Over the next three days we will pick out and explore three of the main themes.

Our first theme (verses 9–13) is that people who follow Jesus will have a tough time. Jesus makes it pretty clear that his followers will get quite a bit of stick. No doubt you've heard of the first Christians being thrown to the lions, and having their bodies covered in tar and set alight as torches for the Roman roads. Grim but true. And Christians are still killed for their faith today.

Jesus makes two great promises to those who follow him. Write them out here.

1. verse 11..

....

2. verse 13..

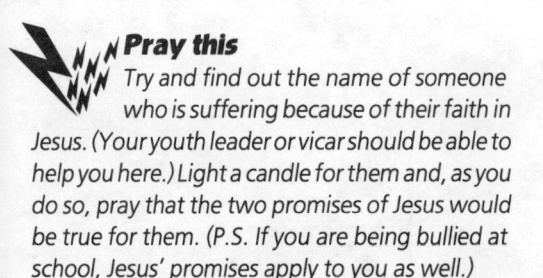

....

Pray this

Try and find out the name of someone who is suffering because of their faith in Jesus. (Your youth leader or vicar should be able to help you here.) Light a candle for them and, as you do so, pray that the two promises of Jesus would be true for them. (P.S. If you are being bullied at school, Jesus' promises apply to you as well.)

Hell on earth

55

Read: Mark chapter 13 verses 14–20

Jesus said, 'For the trouble of those days will be far worse than any the world has ever known... Nor will there ever be anything like it again.'

Mark 13:19

The second theme from this chapter is now history. In AD70, just a few years after Mark wrote his Gospel, Jerusalem was besieged and fell to Titus who became the Roman emperor. That is what Jesus was warning people about here. Everyone who crowded into Jerusalem for safety, rather than running away to the hills, died. It really was hell on earth; 97,000 people were taken captive and 1,100,000 died through starvation or by the sword. The 'awful horror' that Jesus refers to is what the Romans did to God's temple.

Pray this

Towns and cities are under siege in former Yugoslavia and in other parts of the world as I write. Why not find a newspaper article about one of these places, stick it in here and then pray for peace in that place. If you can't find a newspaper, write a prayer for a country that you know is being torn apart by war.

Coming soon

56

Read: Mark chapter 13 verses 21–37

Jesus said, 'No one knows, however, when that day or hour will come—neither the angels in heaven, nor the Son; only the Father knows. Be on watch, be alert, for you do not know when the time will come.'

Mark 13:32–33

When I watch the news or read the paper, I sometimes get very depressed by all the horrific things that people do to each other and the injustice in the world. I wonder why God doesn't do something about it. These verses tell us that God is going to do something about it. One day Jesus will come back and bring the history of our planet as we know it to a close (the end of the world). He will destroy all that is evil and bring everyone who loves him to be with God in heaven.

There may be lots of confusing ideas in these verses but the point of them is that one day Jesus will come back, and though we can never know when, we must always be ready.

ring ring

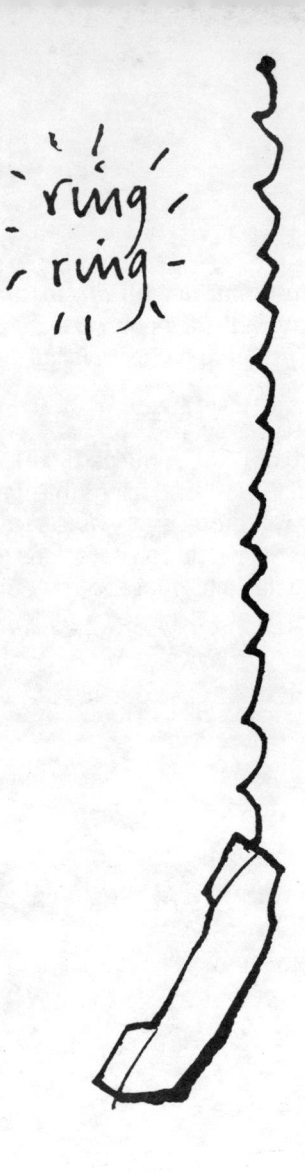

If you knew that at any moment you might get a call from your country's football or netball manager asking you to join the team immediately, you would make sure you were always ready. How would you do that?

1. ....

....

2. ....

....

What do you need to do to make sure that you are always ready for the day when Jesus comes back to take you to be with God?

1. ....

....

2. ....

....

Pray this
Why not ask him to help you keep yourself ready for the big call up?

Love you

57

> Read: Mark chapter 14 verses 1–9
>
> *While Jesus was eating, a woman came in with an alabaster jar full of a very expensive perfume made of pure nard. She broke the jar and poured the perfume on Jesus' head.*
>
> Mark 14:3

This woman's very generous act (splashing out with some perfume that was probably worth a year's wages) was one of the last kind things that was done to Jesus. If you had been there just a few days before Jesus was to sacrifice his life so that you could be forgiven by God, what would you have done to show him how much you loved him? Use this space to tell him about it.

Ponder this
Look back to day 53. Did you give a present to God? How did it go? What will you give him next?

Judas v Jesus

58

Read: Mark chapter 14 verses 10–21

While they were at the table eating, Jesus said, 'I tell you that one of you will betray me—one who is eating with me.'

Mark 14:18

We will never know quite why Judas betrayed Jesus. No doubt greed, jealousy and selfishness all played their part. However, I am more amazed by Jesus' reaction to Judas than Judas' treachery. Jesus could easily have stopped Judas from carrying out his wicked plan either with an army of angels, a thunderbolt from heaven or simply by telling the other disciples exactly what Judas was planning. But he didn't. He simply appealed to Judas to change his mind.

What does this tell you about Jesus?

....

Jesus treats us in the same way. When we choose to do something wrong Jesus doesn't send a thunder-flash angel to wrestle us to the ground as we make for the shop exit with our 'free' Mars bar. Nor does he slap his hand over our mouths as we are about to utter some choice morsels about the class nerd. Instead he taps us on the shoulder and reminds us that what we are about to do perhaps isn't quite worthy of him. It is then up to us to choose.

Ponder this

Can you think of a time when Jesus spoke to you through your conscience like this? What happened? Fill in the bubble and keep listening.

Visual aids

59

Read: Mark chapter 14 verses 22–31
(focus on 22–26)

While they were eating, Jesus took a piece of bread, gave a prayer of thanks, broke it, and gave it to his disciples. 'Take it,' he said, 'this is my body.'

Mark 14:22

If someone is trying to teach you a new skill, like how to change a car wheel, you are far more likely to learn if they actually show you how to do it and then get you to do it yourself, than just tell you how. Jesus understood that, so he explained what his death would mean to his disciples by giving them a visual aid; something that they could see and then do. He said, 'My body will be broken like this bread, and my blood will be shed for you just as this wine is poured out. You will have a fresh start with God if you accept that for yourselves.' Christians still use his visual aid today.

What do the three parts of Jesus' visual aid tell you about the meaning of his death?

1. **Breaking the bread**

   ....
   ....
   ....
   ....

2. **Pouring out the wine**

   ....
   ....
   ....
   ....

3. **Eating and drinking them**

   ....
   ....
   ....
   ....

When we Christians get together to break bread and drink wine, we are using Jesus' visual aid to remind ourselves of how Jesus' body was broken and his blood was shed for us on the cross. Eating a bit of the bread and having a sip of wine is a physical way of saying to God and the other people present, 'I accept Jesus' death for me and want to live for him.'

Ponder this
Next time you are in a church service where bread is broken and wine poured out, remember that they are symbols to remind you that Jesus died for you.

What if...

60

Read: Mark chapter 14 verses 32–42

'Father,' Jesus prayed, 'my Father! All things are possible for you. Take this cup of suffering away from me. Yet not what I want, but what you want.'

Mark 14:36

I find these verses very scary. God asked Jesus to do something very difficult indeed; to sacrifice his life so that you and I could be forgiven. Jesus knew exactly how painful that would be and he also knew that he could save his own bacon by slipping away and never being seen again. What was he to do? It could have gone either way. That may surprise you but Jesus really did have to make the choice.

In this space jot down your thoughts about how your life or the history of the world would have been different if Jesus had said 'No' to God.

Is there no other way?

Pray this
Why not thank Jesus for saying 'Yes'?

Eeeer laddie!

61

Read: Mark chapter 14 verses 43–52

A certain young man, dressed only in a linen cloth, was following Jesus. They tried to arrest him, but he ran away naked, leaving the cloth behind.

Mark 14:51–52

Who was this young lad, just dressed in a night shirt, watching what happened to Jesus? Why does Mark include him in his Gospel? Mysterious eh! Well, people who know better than I, wonder if it might not be Mark himself.

He was the son of a well-off Jerusalem lady who owned the house where the first Christians used to meet and perhaps where Jesus and his disciples held their last supper. He would have been a young lad at the time and maybe he watched the last supper through a crack in the wall and followed Jesus to the garden. Why else would Mark include this otherwise irrelevant event in his book?

Imagine that you are Mark and have crept in late at three a.m. having witnessed all these goings on. What would you write in your diary?

Thursday

....
....
....
....
....
....
....
....
....
....

An honest answer

62

Read: Mark chapter 14 verses 53–65

Again the High Priest questioned Jesus, 'Are you the Messiah, the Son of the Blessed God?' 'I am' answered Jesus.

Mark 14:61–62

I find that being completely honest about myself with other people can sometimes be very difficult because I don't know what the consequences of being honest will be. Thoughts like, 'What will people think? What will happen if I'm really open? Wouldn't it be safer to keep quiet?' pop in and out of my head. Being completely open and honest can be scary. In his 'trial' Jesus was asked the crunch question about himself, 'Are you the Messiah, the Son of God?' An honest answer to that question would have certain consequences—death. However he didn't hesitate to speak the truth despite the massive cost.

Ponder this

Is there anything that you need to be honest with Jesus about? Why not write or talk to him about it now. I promise you that he won't throw up his hands in horror and never speak to you again.

Who?

63

☐

Read: Mark chapter 14 verses 66–72

When the High Priest's servant woman saw Peter warming himself, she looked straight at him and said, 'You too were with Jesus of Nazareth.' But he denied it. 'I don't know... I don't understand what you are talking about,' he answered.

Mark 14:67–68

Last week I took the car to the garage where I have been going for nine years. Steve, the mechanic, asked how my work was going and I happily told him about my painting but I didn't mention the books I was writing to help young people get stuck into the Bible. Why was that? It was because I was nervous about admitting that I was following Jesus. That must be just as upsetting to Jesus as Peter's denial. It is painful reading about Peter because I can see myself in him.

Seeing myself in Peter makes me want to do two things.
1. *Say sorry for past mistakes and start again.*
2. *Wear my friendship with Jesus with pride.*

Ponder this
Do you need to start doing either of these things? Why not chat to Jesus about it. Use this space to jot down your thoughts.

....

....

Ponder this too
Experts think that Mark got his information about the life of Jesus from Peter. Wasn't it honest of Peter to tell Mark about his terrible mistake?!

Paying the price

64

Read: Mark chapter 15 verses 1–20

Pilate spoke again to the crowd, 'What, then, do you want me to do with the one you call the king of the Jews?' They shouted back, 'Crucify him!'

Mark 15:12–13

The injustice and suffering that Jesus experienced were horrific. The crowd was so cruel, and the behaviour of the soldiers so brutal; a crown of thorns, beaten round the head, spat at, mocked. Jesus went through all that for you and me. He took the punishment from God that we deserved for turning our backs on him. He took each blow for each one of us.

On the spikes of this crown of thorns write a few of the wrong things that you have done. Remember that Jesus wore that crown for you and me.

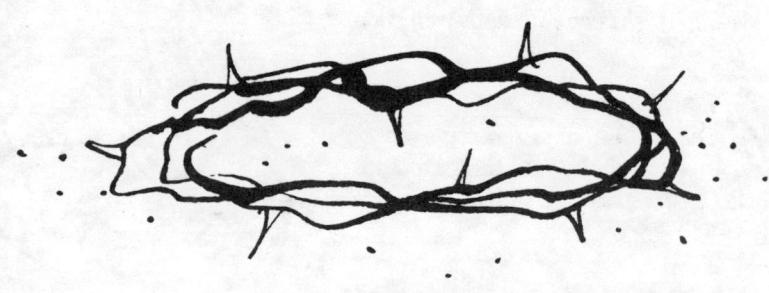

Pray this
Why not thank Jesus for taking the punishment for all the wrong things that you have done and for his never ending love for you.

Love you to death

65

Read: Mark chapter 15 verses 21–32

They took Jesus to a place called Golgotha, which means 'The Place of the Skull'... Then they crucified him.

Mark 15:22, 24

Read the passage again and try and picture the scene; the noises, smells, sounds, and the people present. The chief priests and Jewish leaders believed that they had finally got Jesus, so they taunted him. 'If you're the Messiah, the Son of God,' they said, 'come down from the cross *then* we will believe in you'. Well, Jesus could have come down from the cross but those chief priests wouldn't have believed; they had seen Jesus perform miracles before. More importantly we would have never know how much God loves us. The death of Jesus shows us that God's love is limitless; he was prepared to 'love us to death'.

Ponder this

How do you feel about being loved to death? Jot down you thoughts and share them with Jesus.

Certain conclusions

66

Read: Mark chapter 15 verses 33–41

The army officer who was standing there in front of the cross saw how Jesus had died. 'This man was really the Son of God!' he said.

Mark 15:39

Watching the crucifixion of Jesus was an army officer, who had probably fought in many battles and seen many deaths. Something about the way in which Jesus died was obviously very different, for when he saw it he concluded, 'This man was really the Son of God!'

What do you think it was about Jesus' death that made him say that?

....

....

Ponder this

Has reading about the death of Jesus changed your attitude to Jesus?

Yes ☐   **No** ☐   **Not sure** ☐

If your answer was 'yes', how has your attitude changed? It might help if you looked back to day 34 and to your answer to Jesus' question, 'Who do you say I am?'

....

It's all over

67

> Read: Mark chapter 15 verses 42–47
>
> *Joseph of Arimathea bought a linen sheet, took the body down, wrapped it in the sheet, and placed it in a tomb which had been dug out of solid rock. Then he rolled a large stone across the entrance to the tomb.*
>
> Mark 15:46

Well, it's all over. All the good times, the excitement, the media interest, the dreams, hopes and ambitions are all dead and buried with Jesus. The most exciting three years of the lives of those who followed him have come to terrible end.

What would the devastated disciples write on their master's tomb stone? Inscribe their inscription.

Here is an inscription suggested by Jane Norman aged 13 from Bristol: 'And we thought you were someone special.'

Ponder this
The bravery of Joseph of Arimathea in coming forward to ask for permission to bury Jesus is the only chink of light in the dark events of today's passage. Normally crucifixion corpses would be thrown on the rubbish heap.

Good news!

68

> Read: Mark chapter 16 verses 1–8
>
> *'Don't be alarmed.' the young man said to the women, 'I know you are looking for Jesus of Nazareth, who was crucified. He is not here—he has been raised!... Now go and give this message to his disciples.'*
>
> Mark 16:6–7

It was all over for these women and the disciples. No doubt they were making plans to escape the Jewish authorities and go back to their old lives. But suddenly the most astonishing news breaks into their depression and grief—'JESUS IS ALIVE! He is going to meet you in Galilee. Get your skates on!'

Peter gets a special mention from the angel. He must have been the most depressed of the lot having denied he even knew Jesus. How do you think he would have responded to the women's news. What do you think he would have shouted from the rooftops when he eventually heard it?

Ponder this
How do you respond to the news that Jesus is alive again? Why not talk to God about it.

Approved!

69

Read: Mark chapter 16 verses 9–18

Last of all, Jesus appeared to the eleven disciples.
Mark 16:14

Mark's original ending to his book has been lost, so someone else added verses 9–20 to round it off. They give us a little bit more information about the resurrection and what happened afterwards, which is handy because the resurrection is right at the heart of the Christian faith. By raising Jesus from the dead God showed that he approved of what Jesus had done by his death. The resurrection is God's seal of approval on Jesus' sacrifice.

Design a seal or badge to show that God approves of Jesus' work of forgiveness.

Pray this
Thank you God for approving of Jesus' death in my place and for bringing him back to life again.

Transformed

70

Read: Mark chapter 16 verses 19–20

The disciples went and preached everywhere, and the Lord worked with them and proved that their preaching was true by the miracles that were performed.

Mark 16:20

One of the most convincing bits of evidence for the resurrection of Jesus is the way in which it transformed his disciples. One minute they were depressed and quivering wrecks, the next minute they were out on the streets shouting the good news about Jesus and performing miracles left, right and centre.

Jesus still transforms people today. Whenever someone becomes a Christian, the living Jesus comes to live in them and gradually helps them to become like him. If you are following Jesus then he is transforming you, just as he transformed his first disciples. If you want to start following Jesus all you have to do is ask him to forgive you for ignoring him until now and ask him to start transforming you. Then get some help from another Christian.

Pray this

We do need to cooperate with Jesus if he is to transform us. Use this space to write a prayer asking him to help you play your part in his transformation plans for your life.

....

....

....

A Last Letter

Dear Reader

Well done! You have made it all the way through Mark's Gospel—quite an achievement. To help you see what you have learnt, here are some final questions for you to ponder.

1. Has your attitude to Jesus changed since you started reading Mark?

Yes ☐   No ☐   Not sure ☐

How or why? ....

....

2. What strikes you most about Jesus?

....

....

3. What is the main thing that you have discovered about Jesus?

....

....

Pray this
Why don't you spend some time talking to him about the mark that he has made on you and ask him to make sure that you are marked for life!

Nick

What next?

If you have enjoyed these
'Lightning Bolts' daily readings,
why not get hold of another set?

Other titles in the 'Lightning Bolts' series:

Out of This World
and
Getting to Grips with God

Available soon from your local Christian
bookshop or, in case of difficulty,
direct from BRF: (01865) 748227